First World War
and Army of Occupation
War Diary
France, Belgium and Germany

17 DIVISION
Divisional Troops
Divisional Cyclist Company
13 July 1915 - 31 May 1916

WO95/1991/2

The Naval & Military Press Ltd
www.nmarchive.com
Published in association with The National Archives

Published by

The Naval & Military Press Ltd

Unit 10 Ridgewood Industrial Park,

Uckfield, East Sussex,

TN22 5QE England

Tel: +44 (0) 1825 749494

www.naval-military-press.com

www.nmarchive.com

This diary has been reprinted in facsimile from the original. Any imperfections are inevitably reproduced and the quality may fall short of modern type and cartographic standards.

© Crown Copyright
Images reproduced by permission of The National Archives, London, England, 2015.

Contents

Document type	Place/Title	Date From	Date To
Heading	WO95/1991/2		
Heading	17th Division 17th Divl Cyclist Coy. Jly 1915-May 1916		
Miscellaneous	The Officer Commanding, 17th Divisional Cyclist Company.	29/10/1915	29/10/1915
Miscellaneous	Cyclist Company Seventeenth Division	08/11/1915	08/11/1915
Miscellaneous	17. Co	23/01/1915	23/01/1915
Miscellaneous	II Army. "A".	25/01/1916	25/01/1916
Miscellaneous		24/01/1916	24/01/1916
Heading	British Salonika Force. War Diary.		
Heading	17th Division 17th Divl. Cyclist Coy. Vol I July & August 1915 5 May 16		
Heading	War Diary of The Cyclist Company Seventeenth Division From July 13th 1915 to August 31st 1915 (Volume I)		
War Diary	Southampton	13/07/1915	13/07/1915
War Diary	Havre	14/07/1915	15/07/1915
War Diary	St Omer	15/07/1915	15/07/1915
War Diary	St Martin-Au-Laert	15/07/1915	19/07/1915
War Diary	Terdeghem	19/07/1915	31/07/1915
War Diary	Farm Brandersbeck halfway Between Reninghelst and Westoutre.	01/08/1915	31/08/1915
Heading	17th Division 17th Divl Cyclist Coy Vol II Sept. 15		
Heading	War Diary of The Cyclist Company Seventeenth Division From 1st September 1915 to 30th September 1915 (Volume II)		
War Diary	Farm Brandersbeck halfway between Reninghelst and Westoutre.	01/09/1915	30/09/1915
Heading	17th Division 17th Divl Cyclist Coy Vol 3 Oct 15		
Heading	War. Diary Of Cyclist Company 17th Div. From 1st October. 1915 To 31st October 1915 (Volume)		
War Diary	Farm Halfway Between Reninghelst and Westoutre.	01/10/1915	06/10/1915
War Diary	Winnezeele	06/10/1915	23/10/1915
War Diary	Farm 2 Miles S of Poperinghe	23/10/1915	29/10/1915
Heading	17th Div L. Cyclists Vol 4 Nov 15		
Heading	War Diary Of Cyclist Company 17th Div from. 1st Nov. 1915. to 30th Nov. 1915 (Volume. 5.)		
War Diary	G 19 d 18. (1/40000 28)	01/11/1915	28/11/1915
Heading	17th Div. Cyclist Vol 5		
Heading	War Diary of Cyclist Company 17th Div. From 1st Dec 1915. To 31st Dec. 1915 Volume.		
War Diary	G 19 D 1.8 (Belgium 1/40000 28)	01/12/1915	26/12/1915
Miscellaneous	Cyclists Hounslow		
Miscellaneous	Cyclist Company 17th Division	02/12/1915	02/12/1915
Miscellaneous	Cyclist Coy 17th Div.	02/12/1915	02/12/1915
Miscellaneous	Cyclist Company Seventeenth Division	02/12/1915	02/12/1915
Heading	17 Div Cyclists Jany-May 1916		
Heading	17th Cyclist Vol 6 Jan 1916		
War Diary	G 49d 18 (Belgium 1/40000 Sheet 28)	01/01/1916	04/01/1916
War Diary	Tilques (NW of Stomer)	05/01/1916	27/01/1916

Heading	17th Div Cyclist Coy Vol. 7		
War Diary	Tilques	01/02/1916	07/02/1916
War Diary	Boschepe	11/02/1916	01/03/1916
War Diary	Woodcote House	02/03/1916	02/03/1916
War Diary	Boschepe	03/03/1916	11/03/1916
War Diary	Merris	12/03/1916	21/03/1916
War Diary	Armentiere	21/03/1916	25/03/1916
War Diary	Fromentel 4 1/2 Miles West of Lumbres and 12 West of St Omer	26/03/1916	31/03/1916
War Diary	Fromentel 4 1/2 Miles West Of Lumbres	01/04/1916	10/04/1916
War Diary	Armentieres	10/04/1916	30/04/1916
Heading	17th Div Cyclists Vol 8		
War Diary	Armentieres	01/05/1916	15/05/1916
War Diary	Zudausques	16/05/1916	19/05/1916
War Diary	Moringhem	22/05/1916	24/05/1916
War Diary	Steenwerck	25/05/1916	31/05/1916
War Diary	Armentieres	01/05/1916	15/05/1916
War Diary	Zudausques	16/05/1916	19/05/1916
War Diary	Moringhem	20/05/1916	24/05/1916
War Diary	Steenwerck	25/05/1916	31/05/1916

WO 95/
    /1991 (2)

17TH DIVISION

17TH DIVL CYCLIST COY.

JLY 1915 - MAY 1916.

The Officer Commanding,
14th Divisional Cyclist Company.

To enable me to comply with para 1930 King's Regulations 1912, please forward the following information:-

(i) The Date of Formation of Company.

(ii) Any unusual means by which it was recruited or transfers received.

(iii) The Stations at which it was employed and the dates of its arrival at and departure from such Stations.

(iv) The Military operations in which it has been engaged, and its achievements.

(v) The names of all officers killed and wounded, and the name of any officer or soldier who has specially distinguished himself in action.

(vi) Drafts received and despatched, their strength, dates of their arrival and departure and the names of officers who accompany them. Drafts numerically weaker than an Officer Party should not be separately specified.

(vii) Any other matter which may be considered of historical importance.

HOUNSLOW.   G H Yauw   Major for Colonel
29-10-15   I/C Army Cyclist Corps Records Hounslow.

To 6th Records.
        A.C.C. Hounslow.
Herewith.

                            G W Buckle Capt.
                            for O.C.
                            Cyclist Coy

.2.

CYCLIST COMPANY
SEVENTEENTH DIVISION

To O i/c ARMY CYCLIST CORPS RECORDS
HOUNSLOW, MIDDLESEX

Herewith

(i) The Company was formed on January 23rd 1915

(ii) It was recruited from the Infantry Battalions comprised in the 17th Division viz:-

- 10th West Yorkshire Regt
- 7th Yorkshire Regt
- 7th East Yorkshire Regt
- 6th Dorset Regt } 50th Infantry Brigade

- 7th Lincolnshire Regt
- 10th Sherwood Foresters
- 7th Border Regt
- 8th South Staffordshire Regt } 51st Infantry Brigade

- 9th Northumberland Fusiliers
- 9th W Riding Regt
- 10th Lancashire Fusiliers
- 12th Manchester Regt } 52nd Infantry Brigade

- 7th York and Lancaster Regt — Divisional Troops

All these were "Service" Battalions.

(iii)
Wareham, Dorset — January 23rd – May 27th 1915
On the March — May 27th – May 31st 1915
Winchester, Hants — May 31st – July 13th 1915
In the field with British Expeditionary Force — July 13th – present date

(iv) The Company has been employed with its Division (17th) since July 13th in the operations undertaken by the Division.

(v) No officers killed or wounded
No 4013, Army Cyclist Corps, L/Cpl HANDLEY, W. had his name put forward to the G.O.C. 17th Division for gallant conduct in the trenches when attached to 7th BORDER REGT on 4.10.15.

(VI) a) Before the departure of the Unit from England its numbers were reduced to its War Establishment of 200. Two privates were re-transferred to the 6th Battalion. {2nd Lt W G C LANE and 56 O R were [temporary] transferred to Training Centre, Army Cyclist Corps, Hounslow.

B) In the field drafts have been received from the Training Centre, Army Cyclist Corps, Hounslow as follows:-

 18.9.15   2nd Lt J A PLUMPTON
         3rd CONNAUGHT RANGERS, attached A C C
 5.10.15   7 Privates.
 13.10.15   2 Privates.
 23.10.15   1 L/Cpl and 6 Privates.

VII)   Nil

8.11.15

E W Buckle Capt
for O C Cyclist Company
17th Division

17 .Co.

Formed 23.1.15
Stationed Wareham
 Winchester
arrived France 13 July 15

II Army."A".

In accordance with instructions contained in V Corps letter No. V.A./3522 dated 4.11.15, I forward herewith a statement of ovidence of the circumstances under which Lieut. H.E.Alexander, 17th Cyclist Company, was accidentally wounded as reported in my Casualty Return of 24-1-16.

25/1/16.

A.G.'s OFFICE AT THE BASE
CENTRAL REGISTRY
28 JAN 1916
C. R. No. 18256 B

Major General,
Commanding 17/Division.

A.E. 34.

A.G.
3rd Echelon

Forwarded.

26/1/16

Capt
for General
Comdg. 2/Army

Statement of the circumstances under which Lieutenant H. E. ALEXANDER, Army Cyclist Corps was accidentally wounded by a Mills grenade.

First Evidence — Lieut ALEXANDER states —
I was superintending volley-throwing with bombs at the Divisional School this afternoon and was standing about a yard behind the traverse of the throwing parapet. A piece from one of the bombs struck me and wounded me slightly in the thigh.

Second Evidence — No 3221 Lance-Sergeant T H BOOTMAN, Army Cyclist Corps, states —
I corroborate the above evidence.

Third Evidence — No 4171 Corporal H BECK, Army Cyclist Corps states —
I corroborate the above evidence.

Captain C F VAN DER BYL OC Divisional Grenade School states —
I am of opinion that Lieutenant ALEXANDER was hit by a piece from a bomb which exploded on the top of the parapet which was used as a target for the men to throw over. As Lieutenant ALEXANDER was standing in rear of the traverse of the throwing parapet it is just possible that the fragment may have passed over the top of the parapet, which would have been about five yards from him, and struck him.

24th January 1916.

C. Vander Byl Capt
OC Divisional Grenade
Seventeenth Divis School

BRITISH SALONIKA FORCE.

WAR DIARY.

22 Division

Vol. No.	Unit	From	To
39	C.R.E.	1-2-19	28-2-19
40	99th Field Coy. RE	—	—
40	100th do	—	—
39	127th do	—	—
42	Divisional Signal Coy RE	—	—

121/6874

17th Division

17th Divis: Cyclist Coy:
Vol: I

July & August 1915

15 May 16

CONFIDENTIAL

War Diary

of

The Cyclist Company
Seventeenth Division

from July 13th 1915 to August 31st 1915

(Volume I)

Capt
OC Cyclist Company
17th Division

Army Form C. 2118

13·7·15 – 31·8·15

WAR DIARY
or
INTELLIGENCE SUMMARY
(Erase heading not required.)

Instructions regarding War Diaries and Intelligence Summaries are contained in F. S. Regs., Part II. and the Staff Manual respectively. Title Pages will be prepared in manuscript.

Place	Date	Hour	Summary of Events and Information	Remarks and references to Appendices
SOUTHAMPTON	13/7/15	8.0 PM	Departure of Unit; 7 officers 187 men by S.S. MARGUERITE, 1 officer 5 men and 197 bicycles with transport by S.S. BELLEROPHON	
HAVRE	14/7/15	7.30 AM	Disembarkation	
"	15/7/15	2.30 AM	Visit to trains	
ST OMER	"	10.30 PM	Unit detrains	
ST MARTIN-AU-LAERT	15–18/7/15	–	Billets	
"	18/7/15	–	March to HAZEBROUCK. Billets at BORRE	
"	19/7/15	–	March to TERDEGHEM	
TERDEGHEM	19–31/7/15	–	Billets and continued training	
"	20/7/15	–	In command 6 men attached APM IV Corps ASEELE	
"	31/7/15	–	6 officers and 136 men to form platoons between RENINGHELST and WESTOUTRE. 10 officers and 57 men remain at TERDEGHEM to prepare trenches for grenade school.	
FARM (BRANDERS BECK) halfway between RENING-HELST & WEST-OUTRE	1/8/15 3/8/15	– –	a) Complete reconnaissance made of country carefully attached to trenches b) Digging work done under R.E. c) Divisional Fatigue work near RENING HELST	
"	4/8/15	–	a) 1 officer and 49 men to TERDEGHEM attached to party left 31/7/15. (b) 1 NCO and 7 men attached to APM 17th Division RENINGHELST	
"	5/8/15	–	4 NCOs and 17 men attached to Town Mayor at POPERINGHE	
"	5/8/15	–	3 officers and 106 men return to Company from TERDEGHEM	
"	17/8/15	–	Lieut N KEITH invalided home from off. plat of	
"	26/8/15	–	1 officer and 29 men attached to APM II Corps ANSEELE for duties on road control	
"	31/8/15	–	Strength at 31/8/15 (including men detached) 7 officers, 186 men. 11 bicycles. 2 ASC attached	

1875 Wt. W593/826 1,000,000 4/15 J.B.C. & A. A.D.S.S./Forms/C. 2118.

121/6920

17th Division

17th Brit: Cyclist Coy.
Vol. II

Sept. 15

CONFIDENTIAL

War Diary

of

The Cyclist Company

Seventeenth Division

from 1st September 1915 to 30th September 1915

(Volume II)

L. Van der Byl   Capt
OC Cyclist Company
Seventeenth Division

WAR DIARY or INTELLIGENCE SUMMARY

Army Form C. 2118

Cyclist Company
Seventh Division

Title Pages September 1915

Place	Date	Hour	Summary of Events and Information	Remarks and references to Appendices
FARM (BRANDERS-BEEK) ROAD between RENINGE & WOESTEN	1/9/15		Work a) Reconnaissance of country and roads b) Digging work under R.E. c) Fatigue party under Divisional orders in RENINGHELST	
"	13/9/15			
"	8/9/15		6 men to APM 7th Corps at ABEELE for police duty	
"	9/9/15		1 man to APM 7th Corps at ABEELE in addition to party for Road Control	
"	10/9/15		2nd Lt J.A. Pemberton (3rd Connaught Rangers attached Army Cyclist Corps) join for duty	
"	14/9/15		Fatigue work under R.E.	
"	21/9/15		— (Cyclist Coy R.E.)	
"	21/9/15		Fatigue work under R.E. at Grenade Practice	
"	24/9/15		Company Parade for training	
"	25/9/15		" and Grenade Practice	
"	26/9/15		" "	
"	27/9/15		" — "	
"	28/9/15		One Officer and 35 men return to duty with company from APM 7th Corps at ABEELE	
"	29/9/15		Fatigue work under R.E. and Grenade Practice	
"	30/9/15		"	

12/
7517

17th Division

17th Divl: Cyclist Coy
Vol 3

Oct 15.

CONFIDENTIAL

WAR DIARY
OF
CYCLIST COMPANY 17TH DIV.

FROM 1ST OCTOBER 1915 TO 31ST OCTOBER 1915

(VOLUME)

WAR DIARY or INTELLIGENCE SUMMARY

Army Form C. 2118

Cyclist Company
Seventeenth Division
October 1915

Instructions regarding War Diaries and Intelligence Summaries are contained in F. S. Regs., Part II. and the Staff Manual respectively. Title Pages will be prepared in manuscript.

(Erase heading not required.)

Place	Date	Hour	Summary of Events and Information	Remarks and references to Appendices
FARM midway between RENING[HELST]	1.10.15		Work 1. Fatigue work under R.E. 2. Grenade Practice	
HELST and WESTOUTRE	3.10.15		3. 1 Officer and 17 men attached 7th BORDER REGT in trenches for grenade work 1.10.15 – 4.10.15	
"	4.10.15 5.10.15 6.10.15		Company acts as guides for motor & Brigade company Seventeenth Division	
"	5.10.15	8-9 pm	Reinforcement of seven privates received from Army Cyclist Corps Training Centre	
"	6.10.15		March to WINNEZEELE. 39 men to join unit from Command Duties in 14th V Corps	
WINNEZEELE	6.10.15		Work Training and defence of Division of Grenade school	
"	23.10.15		Move to new Billets Reinforcement of two OR received from Army Cyclist Corps Training Centre Work 1) Duties under R.E. from 28.10.15 2) Preparations for Divisional Grenade school	
FARM 2 miles S of POPERINGHE	23.10.15		10 men attached APM RENINGHELST	
"	23.10.15		Reinforcement of 7 men received from Army Cyclist Corps Training Centre	
"	27.10.15		No 3030 Army Cyclist Corps killed accidentally	
"	29.10.15		38 men attached to APM 5th Corps for Patrol duty (Road)	

1875 Wt. W593/826 1,000,000 4/15 J.B.C. & A. A.D.S.S./Forms/C. 2118.

George W. Smith Capt
for O.C. Cyclist Corp
Seventeenth Division

17ᵗᵉ Stir L: Gebiets
rot: 4

121/7693

Nov. 15

K

CONFIDENTIAL.

War Diary.

of

Cyclist Company   17th Div

From 1st Nov. 1915. to 30th Nov. 1915.

(VOLUME. 5.)

E4 CYCLIST COMPANY
SEVENTEENTH DIVISION WAR DIARY NOVEMBER 1915
INTELLIGENCE SUMMARY

Army Form C. 2118

(Erase heading not required.)

Instructions regarding War Diaries and Intelligence Summaries are contained in F. S. Regs., Part II. and the Staff Manual respectively. Title Pages will be prepared in manuscript.

Place	Date	Hour	Summary of Events and Information	Remarks and references to Appendices
J 19 d L 8 (Sheet 28)	1.11.15 to 4.11.15		Working party under R.E. daily in SANCTUARY WOOD. Preparation of Divisional GRENADE SCHOOL	
"	5.11.15		Working party on Reserve Trenches near VLAMERTINGHE. Preparation and announcement of Divisional GRENADE SCHOOL	
"	21.11.15		Commencement of Divisional Grenade Technical School	
"	26.11.15		20 men attached Town MAJOR, POPERINGHE	
	28.11.15		Working party on Reserve trenches etc.	

1875 Wt. W593/826 1,000,000 4/15 J.B.C. & A. A.D.S.S./Forms/C. 2118.

17th Mil: Collect.
Vol: 5

121/
7935

CONFIDENTIAL.

War Diary.

of

Cyclist Company 17th Div.

From 1st Dec 1915.   To 31st Dec. 1915.

VOLUME.

CYCLIST COMPANY
SEVENTEENTH DIVISION

WAR DIARY or INTELLIGENCE SUMMARY

Army Form C. 2118

DECEMBER 1915

Place	Date	Hour	Summary of Events and Information	Remarks and references to Appendices
19 d 1:8 (Boisleux Town 28)	1.12.15		Work in connection with Divisional Technical School, 17th Division (Fatigues)	
	10.12.15		Lt W TEED, 2nd Lt J A PLUMPTON and 61 O.R. attached 51st Infantry Brigade (1 8 e s 10)	
	12.12.15		No 2133 Pte SISSEN T wounded	
	19.12.15		Party attached to 51st Infantry Brigade in gas attack at YPRES and subsequent bombardment	
			2nd Lt TAPLUM OTON wounded (shell shock)	
			Captain BUCKLE attached 51st Infantry Brigade for Lt W TEED (20 men relieved)	
	21.12.15		2nd Lt C C G SMITH attached 51st Infantry Brigade	
	26.12.15		Lt H E ALEXANDER attached 51st Infantry Brigade for Capt G W BUCKLE (20 men relieved)	

SECRET.

A.G.'s OFFICE AT THE BASE
CENTRAL REGISTRY
14 JAN 1916
C. R. No. 70/787

The Officer i/c Records

Cyclists – Hounslow.

I forward herewith for safe custody in a parcel, numbered as is letter, the following documents :-

Statements re loss of bicycles.

The above are the property of :-

O.C. Cyclist Co. 17th Divn.

KINDLY ACKNOWLEDGE RECEIPT.

(Sgd) J. Scott. Major

General Head Quarters.
3rd Echelon.

(for) D. A. G. 3rd Echelon.

CYCLIST COMPANY
17th DIVISION

On 6th October 1915 this Unit marched from RENINGHELST, BELGIUM to WINNEZEELE, FRANCE.

In consequence of lack of space on the transport of the Unit it was necessary to leave two Government bicycles behind. They were shewn to the Unit taking over the billets (Grenade School, 24th Division) who were asked to give them to the Cyclist Coy. 24th Division who were to billet near.

These bicycles (Trade Nos 198785 and 199243 Collapsible pattern) were the worst in the Unit's possession and in very poor repair.

G W Buerdle Capt.
for O C Cyclist Coy.
17 Div.

2-12-15

To OC. Cyclist Coy
17th Div.

Sir,

On July 26th I was engaged upon road reconnaissance round STEENVOORDE.

At 9-0 am I procured the use of a room at the Headquarters of the 1st Battn. Royal West Kent Regt to explain what was required of the men I was working, leaving the cycles outside. The men departed on their various duties and five minutes later I followed.

I then found my cycle to be missing.

I sent men out in search of it and informed the men on police duty in STEENVOORDE but no trace of it could be found.

H Luleman
2nd Lieut
Cyclist Coy
17 Div.

26th Nov. 15

This bicycle was of collapsible pattern. Trade number 199580 No 125 on plate No 321 on mudguard

The loss was advertised without result in Divisional Routine Orders of 2/8/15.

2-12-15

GW Buckle Capt.
for OC
Cyclist Coy
17 Div.

Cyclist Company
Seventeenth Division
—

On 6th November 1915 I was stationed at BUSSEBOOM as orderly for the 17th Divisional Cyclist Company with the RE Signal Company Seventeenth Division. About 11·0 AM I returned with my bicycle from delivering a message and left my bicycle with some others outside the office while I went in. About 2·15 PM I was sent on another message and on coming out I found that my bicycle was no longer there. There were two or three bicycles still there and mine was the only one missing.

Signed AE Smith. Pte
No 4024 Army Cyclist Corps.

This loss was advertised in Divisional Orders of 8·11·15 without success. The bicycle was of collapsible pattern. Trade number 199604. No 371 on rear mudguard. No 146 on plate.

G W Buckle Capt
for OC Cyclist Coy
17th Division

2·12·15

17 DuCyclots
Jany – April
1916

12th Cyclic
Vol: 6
Paris 1816.

WAR DIARY or INTELLIGENCE SUMMARY

Army Form C. 2118

CYCLIST COMPANY SEVENTEENTH DIVISION

(Erase heading not required.)

JANUARY 1916

Place	Date	Hour	Summary of Events and Information	Remarks and references to Appendices
G.H.Q d.18 (Belgium/French Sheet 28)	1.1.16		Lt ALEXANDER, 2nd Lt SMITH and detachment from duty with 51st Infantry Brigade at YPRES	
"	2.1.16		2nd Lt SMITH and detachment proceed to TILQUES (N.W. of ST OMER)	
"	3.1.16		COMPANY march to ZERMEZEELE	
"	4.1.16		Company march to TILQUES (N.W. of ST OMER)	
TILQUES (N.W. of ST OMER)	5.1.16		26 men from Trestler Control Yt Corps and 20 men from Town. Major POPERINGHE rejoin. Draft of 3 received	
"	6.1.16		Return of New Divisional Technical School	
"	7.1.16		8 men attached Divisional Claims Officer	
"	16.1.16		2 men received as Draft	
"	17.1.16		1st Divisional Technical School begins	
"	18.1.16		Draft of 7 men received	
"			Cyclist Company marches past G.O.C 2nd Army	
"	24.1.16		Temporary Lt H.E. ALEXANDER slightly wounded accidentally by portion of grenade	
"	27.1.16		Temporary Lt H.E. ALEXANDER return to duty	
"	28.1.16		Draft of 14 men received	

17th Div.
Cyclist Coy
Vol. 7

CYCLIST COMPANY
SEVENTEENTH DIVISION WAR DIARY
or
INTELLIGENCE SUMMARY
(Erase heading not required.)

Army Form C. 2118

Instructions regarding War Diaries and Intelligence Summaries are contained in F.S. Regs., Part II. and the Staff Manual respectively. Title Pages will be prepared in manuscript.

Place	Date	Hour	Summary of Events and Information	Remarks and references to Appendices
TILQUES	1.2.16		Company Training	
	5.2.16			
	5.2.16		Moved to MORINGHEM	
	6.2.16		Moved to STAPLE	
	7.2.16		Moved to BOESCHEPE	
BOESCHEPE	11.2.16		Temp/Lt HE ALEXANDER and 43 OR Left Adj with 18th CORPS	
"	15.2.16		Temp/Capt GW BUCKLE, Temp/2nd Lt WHARMOURS W SALMON and 96 OR attached to 51st BRIGADE at the BLUFF	
			Temp/Capt Lt W SALMON and Party took part in bombing Action under 51st Infantry BRIGADE. Two men wounded	
			and one slightly wounded. Temp/Lt KC EG SMITH and 12 men attached 17th Division HQ for guide duties	
	16.2.16		Temp/2nd Lt CNC FIELD joins Unit.	
			Party from 51st Infantry Brigade rejoin Unit. Also 2nd Lt SMITH and guides again	
	21.2.16		No 3229 Pte WND JS died of wounds	
	21.2.16			
	25.2.16		Travel diagrams under orders 17th Division	

June

Army Form C. 2118

CYCLIST COMPANY
SEVENTEENTH DIVISION
MARCH 1916

WAR DIARY
or
INTELLIGENCE SUMMARY
(Erase heading not required.)

Instructions regarding War Diaries and Intelligence Summaries are contained in F. S. Regs., Part II. and the Staff Manual respectively. Title Pages will be prepared in manuscript.

Place	Date	Hour	Summary of Events and Information	Remarks and references to Appendices
BOESCHEPE	1/3/16	6 P.M	CAPT. G.W. BUCKLE, 2nd LT. CE. SMITH and 1st LT. CNCFIELD and 26 men to WOODCOTE HOUSE to form escort for prisoners of late taken. Party of 6 trained guides attached to Division.	
WOODCOTE HOUSE	2/3/16	—	4 Prisoner Officers and 228 men forwarded to A.P.M. 17th Division. 1 officer and 14 men moved next to Field Dressing Station. These prisoners were taken in the recapture of the BLUFF and afterwards handed to 10 men to WOODCOTE HOUSE as escort relief	
BOESCHEPE	3/3/16	—	Party from WOODCOTE HOUSE return	
"	10/3/16		March to MERRIS south west of BAILLEUL	
METEREN	12/3/16		1st Lt. ALEXANDER and detachment released from employment with IInd Corps	
"	14/3/16		Training	
"	21/3/16		March to ARMENTIERES.	
ARMENTIERES	21/3/16		8 n.c.o's and 24 men for grenade on trenches west of ARMENTIERES.	
"	22/3/16		This detachment was released from duty on Bridge 4 men and 18 men attached to A.P.M. 17th Div. for duty.	
"	24/3/16 – 9/4/16		COMPANY (17th Division) moved to RENESCURE under 2nd Cavalry Division	
"	25/3/16	—	COMPANY arrive at FROMENTEL for training	
FROMENTEL	26/3/16		Training in duties of Divisional Mounted Troops carried out under arrangements of 2nd Cavalry Division will Divisional Squadron of mounting	
LUMBRES			(A Squadron (Queen's own YORKSHIRE DRAGOONS)	
NEWEST BRACHT	31/3/15			
LUMBRES				

1875 Wt. W593/826 1,000,000 4/15 J.B.C. & A. A.D.S.S./Forms/C. 2118.

Army Form C. 2118

17th Cyclist
Vol 9

WAR DIARY
or
INTELLIGENCE SUMMARY

(Erase heading not required.)

Instructions regarding War Diaries and Intelligence
Summaries are contained in F. S. Regs., Part II.
and the Staff Manual respectively. Title Pages
will be prepared in manuscript.

C¹-21ST COMPANY SEVENTEENTH BATTALION

Place	Date	Hour	Summary of Events and Information	Remarks and references to Appendices
FREMENTEL	1/4/16		Having left Oxford Squadron of Yeomanry and the Machine Gun Section preceded Part of	
Headquarters	2/4/16			
	9-4-16		Moved to LEMERLE (t d'ARGOES)	
	10-4-16		Moved to ARMENTIÈRES	
	21-4-16			

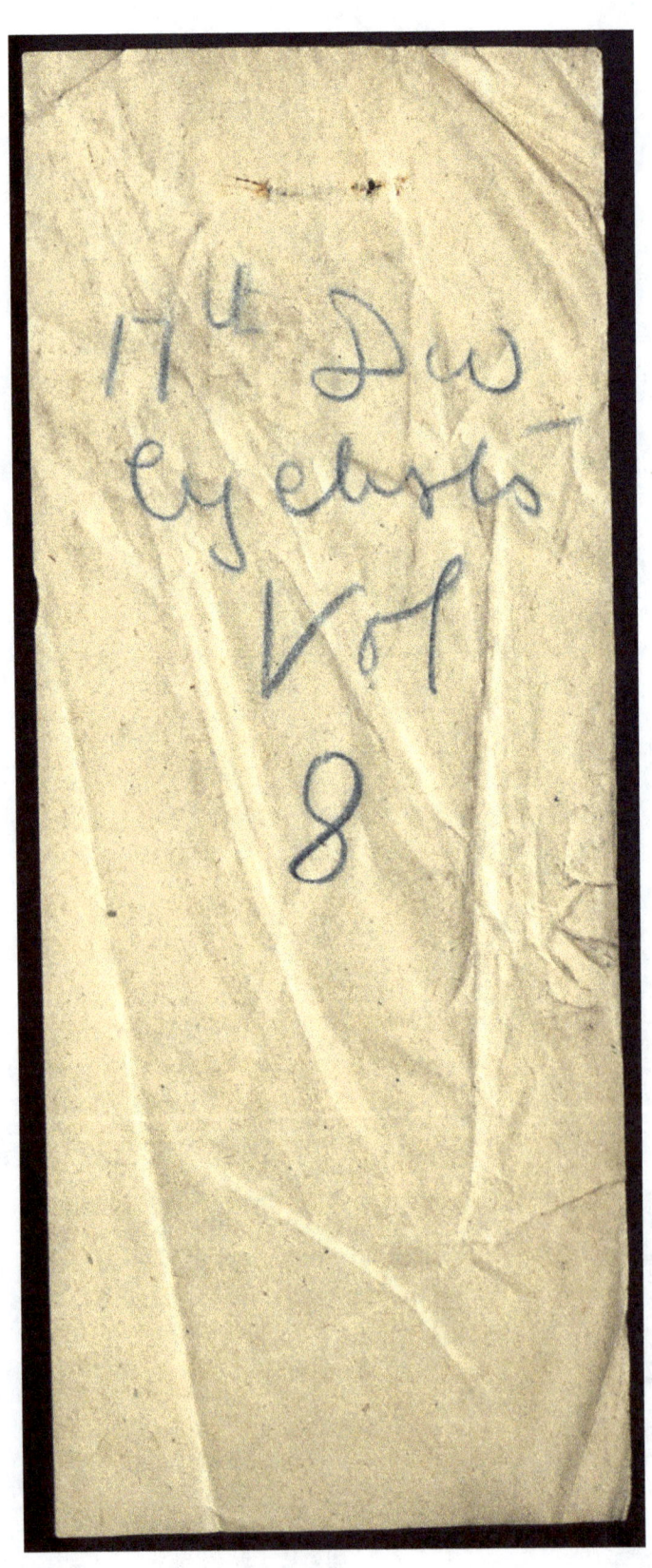

17th Dec
eyedrops
Vol
8

Army Form C. 2118

238

WAR DIARY
or
INTELLIGENCE SUMMARY
(Erase heading not required.)

CYCLIST COMPANY, SEVENTEENTH DIVISION

MAY 1916

Place	Date	Hour	Summary of Events and Information	Remarks and references to Appendices
ARMENTIERES	1.5.16 – 14.5.16		Miscellaneous divisional employment	
	15.5.16		March to ZUDAUSQUES	
ZUDAUSQUES	16.5.16		Marais practice trenches for Division	
	18.5.16			
	19.5.16		March to MOLINGHEM	
MOLINGHEM	22.5.16		79 O.R. transferred to 9th Batt. the W. Riding Regt.	
	23.5.16		67 surplus bicycles returned to Ordnance	
"	24.5.16		6 O.R. transferred to 9th Batt. the W. Riding Regt.	
—			2 Officers and S O R transferred to No 3 Base Infantry Depot	
			March to STEENWERCK	
STEENWERCK	25.5.16		Incorporation of Unit in 2nd Corps Cyclist Battalion	
	30.5.16			
	31.5.16		March to RENESCURE	

G. M. Brunel Capt.

WAR DIARY or INTELLIGENCE SUMMARY

Army Form C. 2118

CYCLIST COMPANY, SEVENTEENTH DIVISION

MAY 1918

Place	Date	Hour	Summary of Events and Information	Remarks and references to Appendices
ARNEKE	1.5.18 – 14.5.18		Miscellaneous Divisional Employment	
	15.5.18		March to ZUDAUSQUES	
ZUDAUSQUES	16.5.18 – 12.5.18		Making practice trenches for Division	
	19.5.18		March to MONINGHEM	
MONINGHEM	22.5.18		79 O.R. transferred to 9th Batt. the W Riding Regt	
"	23.5.18		67 cyclists bicycles returned to Ordnance	
	24.5.18		6 O.R. transferred to 9 R Batt the W Riding Regt. 2 Officers and 5 O R transferred to No 3 Base Infantry depot	
	27.5.18		March to STEENWERCK	
STEENWERCK	28.5.18 – 30.5.18		Incorporation of Units in 2nd Corps Cyclist Battalion	
	31.5.18		March to RENESCURE	

www.ingramcontent.com/pod-product-compliance
Lightning Source LLC
Chambersburg PA
CBHW081459160426
43193CB00013B/2534